KU-041-504

Contents

Why does art matter? 4
Be an arts administrator 6
Be an animator 8
Be an art therapist 10
Be a photographer 12
Be an exhibition designer 14
Be a fashion designer 16
Be a fine artist 18
Be an interior designer 20
Be a graphic designer 22
Be an illustrator 24
Choosing the right job for you 26
Art job chart 28
Glossary 30
Find out more 31
Index 32

Some words are shown in bold, **like this**. You can find out what they mean by looking in the glossary.

Why does art matter?

Do you love art? Or do you wonder what the point of art is? Art is important in the world around us. We see art every day, even if we don't notice it!

We see art around us all the time, often where we don't expect it.

If art is your favourite activity, then you might like to get a job that involves art. Read this book to find out about some great jobs that involve art. Could one of them be for you?

Be an arts administrator

If you were an arts administrator, your job might be to organize art activities for people. You might talk to artists about displaying their work. You could work in a **gallery** and arrange art activities for visitors.

Arts administrators help artists to share their work with the public.

Arts administrators help to organize new exhibitions.

Arts administrators need to tell people about art **exhibitions** and events. They need to be very interested in art and know a lot about it. Arts administrators have to be very organized and good at talking to people.

Be an animator

If you love watching cartoons, you might like to be an animator. You would make films that tell a story using moving pictures or models. Your animations could be on television, on computer games, or on websites.

Animators need to be very careful and patient.

Some animators have their own ideas for films and write the stories themselves. They have to plan how each **character** and **scene** will look. Many animators use computers to make their films.

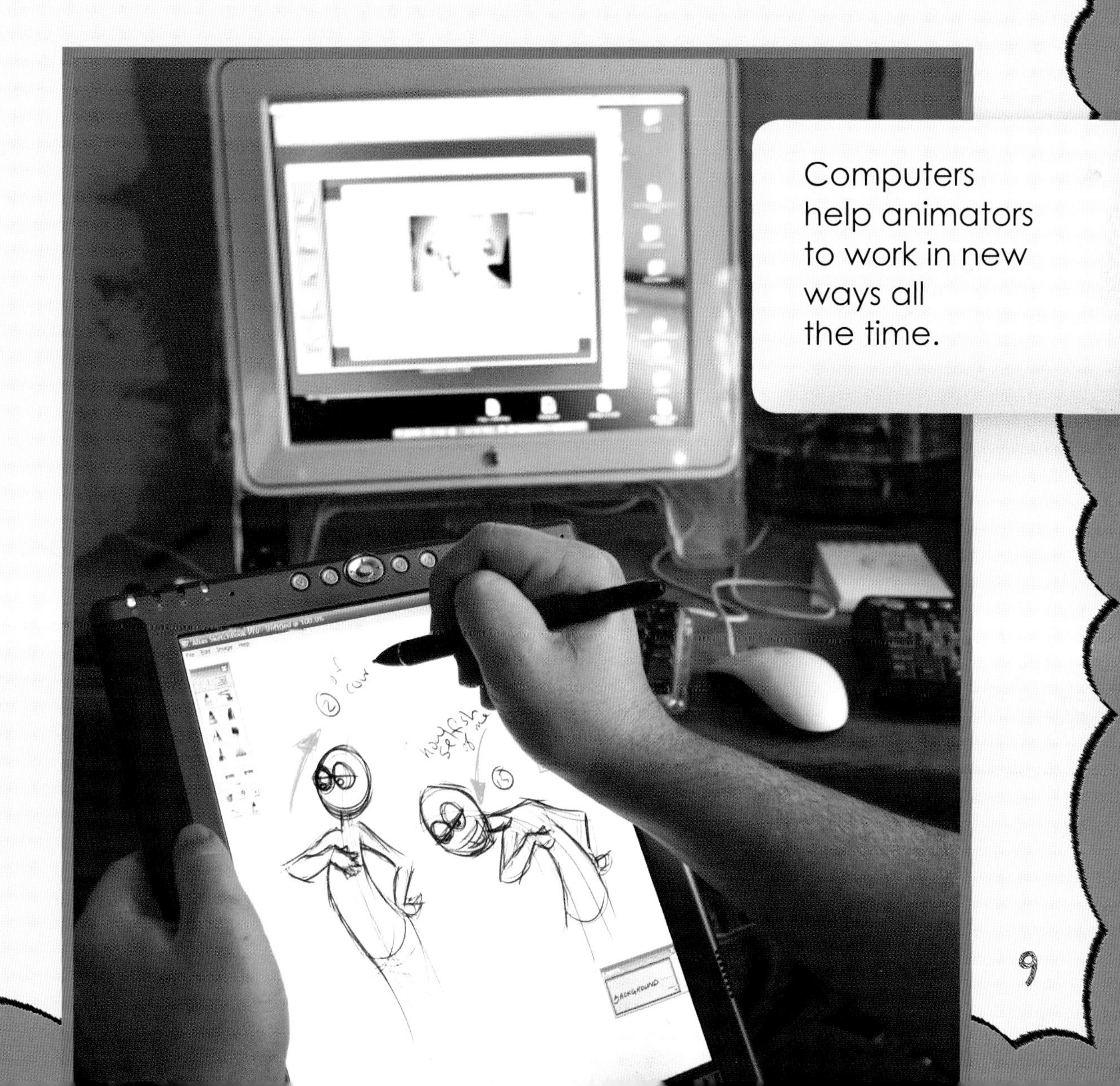

Computers help animators to work in new ways all the time.

Be an art therapist

If you were an art **therapist**, you would use art to make people feel better. You would show them how to use different materials and **techniques** to make paintings, drawings, and **sculptures**.

Art therapists help people to work through their problems by making art.

Making art can be a good way to relax and feel better.

Art therapists work with children or adults who are ill or unhappy. They need to be good at making art in lots of different ways. Therapists also need to be good at talking and listening to people.

Be a photographer

If you enjoy taking photos then you might like a job as a photographer. You might take photographs for newspapers and websites. Or you could take school photographs or wedding pictures.

You could be a fashion photographer.

Some photographers need to be good at helping people to relax and enjoy having their photograph taken.

Photographers often use lots of **equipment**, such as special lighting. Photographers also sometimes use computers to **retouch** photographs.

Be an exhibition designer

If you were an **exhibition** designer, your job would be to come up with ideas for **displays** at **conferences** and exhibitions. The displays tell people who is there and what they do.

People visit conferences and exhibitions to share ideas and try to work with other people.

Exhibition designers start by talking to people about what they want their display to look like. Then they make sketches, draw plans on a computer, or make models. When everyone is happy, they build the display.

Exhibition designers need to be good at listening to people and explaining how things will look.

Be a fashion designer

If you are interested in clothes and **accessories**, you might like to be a fashion designer. Fashion designers have new ideas for how clothes are worn or look. They experiment with new shapes, patterns, and **fabrics**.

Fashion designers are always looking for new ways to wear clothes.

Fashion designers need to be good at art to see how clothes can look good.

Some fashion designers make very expensive, **designer clothes**. Others make clothes that most people buy in the shops. Some fashion designers make sportswear or clothes for children.

Be a fine artist

If you are very good at drawing and painting, you might like to be a fine artist. You could make **sculptures** or **prints**. People would see your best work in a **gallery** and sometimes buy it.

Fine artists are very skilled at using different materials to make art.

Some sculptures can become part of the landscape.

Sometimes people ask artists to make a special piece of art. These pieces of art can be displayed in public spaces. Other artists work in schools to help children make art.

Be an interior designer

If you were an interior designer, you would think about the inside of buildings. You might design the inside of people's homes, offices, shops, or other buildings. You could change the design of old buildings or have ideas for brand new buildings.

Interior designers are always looking for new ideas.

Interior designers start by talking to people about what they want. They may sketch some ideas and think about colours, furniture, and **fabrics**. Then they organize the decoration of the building.

Some interior designers use computers or make models to plan rooms.

Be a graphic designer

If you were a graphic designer, you would use a computer to work with pictures and words. You might design websites, books, or magazines. Some graphic designers create text and pictures for television or adverts.

Graphic designers are very skilled at using computers.

Graphic designers work to turn people's ideas into images and pictures.

Graphic designers have to give people information in a way they will notice. They need to be good at using computers and have lots of good ideas. Graphic designers know which colours and shapes work well together.

Be an illustrator

If you enjoy drawing then you might like to be an illustrator. Some illustrators draw or paint pictures for stories or book covers. Other illustrators create pictures for schoolbooks or magazines. Some illustrators draw pictures for instructions and leaflets.

Many illustrators still use pencils and paints to create their pictures.

Illustrators need to work in a **style** that is right for the people who see the pictures. Pictures in stories might be colourful and bright. Illustrations on an instruction leaflet would be clear and simple.

Many illustrators use computers to make their illustrations.

Choosing the right job for you

When you decide what you want to do when you are older, don't just think about school subjects. Think about what you enjoy doing. If you like helping people then you might like to be an art **therapist**.

If you love films and cartoons, you might enjoy working in animation. There are so many exciting jobs that use art that there is something to suit everyone.

Five things you couldn't do without art

- Read comics
- Play computer games
- Wear cool clothes
- Watch cartoons
- Take photos of your friends

Art job chart

If you want to find out more about any of the jobs in this book, start here:

	Animator	Arts administrator	Art therapist	Exhibition designer
You need to:	Be very patient	Know a lot about art	Be good at talking and listening to people	Be able to work quickly and carefully
Best thing about it:	Seeing a finished film!	Helping people to see and enjoy art!	Helping someone feel better!	Seeing your displays stand out!

	Fashion designer	Fine artist	Graphic designer	Illustrator	Interior designer	Photographer
	Love fashion	Be very good at art	Be good at using words and pictures to get people's attention	Know how to use pictures to give people information	Know what colours and shapes look good together	Know how to use lots of equipment
	Seeing people look good in your clothes!	Doing what you love every day!	Creating designs that people love!	Seeing people enjoy your finished work!	Seeing people enjoy using a finished room!	Looking at fantastic photos!

Glossary

character person in a story, play, or film
conference meeting held for lots of people
designer clothes clothes that are expensive and in a style that no one else has
display arrangement of things to be shown
equipment something made to be used in a special way
exhibition place where pieces of art and artefacts are displayed for people to look at
fabric cloth or material
gallery place where paintings and sculptures are displayed
print art made by transferring ink onto a surface
retouch make something look a bit better
scene the surroundings during part of a film or play
sculpture 3-dimensional (3D) art made by moulding, carving, welding, or cutting a material
style way in which something is made or done
technique special way of doing something
therapist person who is trained to help people using special treatment

Find out more

Design Council
www.designcouncil.org.uk/about-design/Types-of-design/
Find out about all types of design on this website.

Aardman
www.aardman.com/about-us/studio-tour/
Visit this website for a tour of Aardman animation studios and see what different people do to help create an animated film.

The House of Illustration
www.houseofillustration.org.uk/
Find out more about illustration on this website.

Index

accessories 16
animators 8–9, 27, 28
arts administrators 6–7, 28
art therapists 10–11, 26–27, 28

buildings 20, 21

cartoons 8, 27
characters 9
clothes 16–17, 27, 29
computers 8, 9, 13, 15, 22, 23, 27
conferences 14

designer clothes 17
displays 14–15, 19, 28

equipment 13, 29
exhibition designers 14–15, 28
exhibitions 7, 14, 28

fabrics 16, 21
fashion designers 16–17, 29
fine artists 6, 18–19, 29

galleries 6, 18
graphic designers 22–23, 29

illustrators 24–25, 29
importance 4, 27
interior designers 20–21, 29

photographers 12–13, 29
photographs 12, 13
plans 9, 15

retouching 13

scenes 9
schools 19, 24, 26

techniques 10